Watch

Bill Wootton

Watch

GP

Thanks

Thank you to members of Ross Gillett's weekly poetry workshops in Daylesford, who have seen early versions of many of these poems and particular thanks to Ross for his guidance.

Thanks also to regular commentators and contributors to the online journal *poetryetc*, especially Sheila Murphy, the late Douglas Barbour, Jill Jones, Andrew Burke and Patrick McManus.

My ventures into haiku and senryu owe much to the generosity of Myron Lysenko.

Sandi Nicolaides read and engaged with many of these poems in draft form and I appreciate her encouragement.

My wife Chris Wootton has been a valuable sounding board and she picked up many a clunk I would have missed.

Watch
ISBN 978 1 76109 521 4

Cover image: Peter Slingsby

First published 2023 by
GINNINDERRA PRESS
PO Box 3461 Port Adelaide 5015
www.ginninderrapress.com.au

Contents

The driveway

When I was young
the driveway of my mind uncoiled
straight as any tongue
and leaves blew across it

The breeze tugged me out
tore me loose and pointed
away, far away

I want to come back now
and smell the jasmine
ask if my Superball
has turned up
I want to tread the concrete

Watch

Face the size of the newly released ten-cent bit
the watch Grandma Beat gave me for my tenth birthday
was just right for my narrow wrist

A thin red second hand jerked over solid black numbers
Luminous lime on skeletal gold
outlined the prime movers

The brown leather band was stiff and the buckle flimsy
but whizzo was its presentation in a crimson Bevilles box
which closed with a soft huff

Long ago the watch was left in a squash change room
but the box is still in fine order
home to badges also once worn

No Nukes The Clash Legalise it
and already obsolete –
a pea-green iPod nano

Time back then was on everybody's hands
Pre-digital creatures we were
Wrist ready

Does it mean anything now to tap
on your forearm interrogatively?
Grandma Beat ran out of time a year after gifting me

The old box having seen off its ticker within
may yet outlive
its worn wearer

My very own golden pond

Grade two, felt the urge
Full bladder, must purge

In class, what to do
Can't just leave room

Couldn't ask, no one did
I was just – a kid

Cross legs, hang on
But I knew – I was gone

Left leg feeling warm
First trickle absorbed

Black serge short pants,
Inside something shrank

Oh no, on the floor
Small puddle starts to form

Face flushes full red
Dignity, no shred

Socks damp, shoes full
Ready for ridicule

But all round, no one stirs
Teacher says not a word

Eons pass, don't dare shift
Should I use my handkerchief?

When, finally, the bell…
To the door I squelch

Once there, still not free
Dark footprints dog me

Mid-lunch, I stare
Mop and bucket in there

Thank you, someone –
My lake expunged

Change

In come the dollars
In come the cents

Waiting for the yellow bus

to replace the pounds
the shillings and the pence

Fingering a battered sixpence

Something
something or other
thrown into the mix
on the 14th of February 1966

and here it is –

No dour pennies
clank to hand
Change is a button-
sized one-cent bit
lightweight and gleaming
with the wide eyes
of a feathertail glider
front and centre
and big brother two cents
boasting a panicked frill-necked lizard

Sure Queenie is still there
on the flip side
but these coins feel Australian
and up-to-the-minute

Soon to surface will be silver echidna fives
lyrebird tens and platypus twenties
but the copper promise
of what would later be termed shrapnel
demonstrated that change
was not only possible
it was here

At the crossing

Two pharmacies faced off in East Ivanhoe
one press of a red rubber button away

Two kids prepared to cross
neither aware of the breathing quality of the other

The girl looked straight ahead
The boy's neck fished

At green the girl took a step
The boy's eyes tracked a yellow flash

Legs followed hard upon
The girl took back her step

opened her mouth
shut it just

as the yellow bus door folded
the boy within

Environment

i

Why don't you go and play outside
less a question than a Mum instruction
to *Jungle-Jim*-on-TV-watching-me

Before Environment, there was outside
Land of apricot trees, grass, concrete, sky
Monochromed eyes adjust blinkingly to colour

Pick up a footy from under the clothesline
Bounce it a few times. What would Bomba do?
Where are the swinging vines?

ii

Tarzan lived outside, even slept in trees
I felt more outside watching him and safari-suited men
with pith helmets than in the backyard

Ah-woo, ah wooh woo wooh
mysterious deep African jungle sound
I find out later was a kookaburra

But ex-Olympian Johnny Weissmuller
did all his own swimming stunts
and patented his yell for all Tarzans to come

iii

Backyard cluttered with excess from inside
What's this cracked tabletop doing out here?
Best deal with it with this old hammer

Now what? Bit junglier down the side
Ah, fuchsias. Tear off a branchlet
Fold it near the flower, aim and shoot

In between the tool shed and the garage
squelch through solid wandering Jew
to the fence – end of my outside

iv

How did that marble top get smashed?
Dad demanded after work
Just going outside to play, Mum

Kite

When Mum was in hospital Dad made us a kite.
It was diamond-shaped.
First he made a cross out of light wood scraps.
Then he wrapped brown paper around it somehow.
String was involved too.
And torn cloth pieces for the tail.

In each corner Dad carefully
inked our names in texta.
Me, top left, brother Dan top right,
Jim for Dad and bottom right, Bob,
the brother to be brought home.
Dan was not happy. Bob
had not yet earned his stripes.

We waited for a windy day.
Got one. Hared off after school
up to the oval at Ivanhoe Grammar.
I carried the kite, Dan the bit of wood
with string wound round it in figure 8s.
How was it attached to the kite?
Can't remember.
At the crossbars I suppose.

I do remember Dan and I took turns
to run full tilt dragging the kite behind
hoping for a kick of breeze to catch
and jerk it up.
All we managed mostly
was to burble it along a bit
before it grubbed to grass.

The day it did get up
it took some holding
until high up in the air,
the rip,
the slackening,
the plunge.

Maybe Dad tried a repair job.
Doubtful.
I seem to recall it lying
in the woodshed
mouldering.
No good asking Bob.

But at least once we passed
the string baton from hand to hand.
The tail sort of worked,
flickering about,
and as the kite continued to rise
our names retreated into illegibility.

The footy

Taking it in turns
to run a kick's length ahead,
brother Dan and I
short-passed and marked
the brand-new red leather Sherrin
all the way up Robin Hood Road.

Neither of us had dared to believe
the prize we'd won for filling out a coupon
to say why we liked White Wings flour
in ten words or less, would be
an actual footy.
Plastic, we assumed.

But Jack O'Sullivan the grocer
calmly reached beneath the till
and presented us with
real leather and laces.
We each signed
and shot out the door.

Turning right on the home stretch
down Wallis Avenue,
Dan positioned himself to be
the receiver outside our house
so he could be the first
to rush in and show Mum.

wagging

no history
after lunch
for the first time

sitting on paspalum
under the clothesline
in Jimmy B's backyard

the rest have drifted back for maths
leaving just Dolores and me

she reaches over
scoops up a soft pack
flicks the bottom
shakes up a pure white Kent
lips it out

pauses
plucks out the unlit cigarette

do you think people
talk
when they're
you know
doing it?

the pegs above
tighten their grip
on Jimmy's singlets

Paperbark in the nature strip

Out the front of the Ivanhoe house we rented,
a melaleuca *linariifolia* stood in the nature strip,
one of a string of half a dozen or so: paperbarks.

Half-peeling flaps of white bark straggled from it,
each thinner than a cigarette paper. Like a big broccoli,
dense, creamy white flowers clumped in its canopy.

But the flowers were way up high. Through the sash
window in the front bedroom only the trunk appeared
as I groped for undergraduate sentences.

Words required pulling from my fettered mind.
Often they stayed as stuck as the dirty white bark
on that tree, as wind whistled down Livingstone Street.

None of us had a motor mower but a push-job
was good enough for the nature strip even if
it was a hairy proposition on the busy road side,

involving street stepping around the scruffy girth.
By the end of Honours year, no mower would fit
and the grass had to be clipped or stay shaggy.

The Cal Bung house has long bitten the dust now.
Units, at least six, splay out on the old block.
But the paperbark has only firmed its claim.

The circumference of the trunk is now such
that no grass can be seen on the road side
or the footpath side and the concrete kerbing

has cracked. I've fallen at the doctorate hurdle
but forty years down the track, the paperbark
looks like claiming a bitumen prize.

senryu 1

iron armour
for those
sharp creases

The man with the koala tattoo.
That's it. What further
details do you require?

after a haircut
do you too
use a little less shampoo?

Back tracking

Afternoon, a Doctors Gully stroll.
Behind an abandoned guest house
a stony path curls
before broadening into a surprise
slashed grass track.
Pass under tall manna gums, the odd sycamore.
Among them appears a redgum,
a lumpy-trunked, unfinished-looking river redgum.
What's that sound?
Not psithurism.
Bees massing.

A sidetrack dips
to an unslashed, earthen creek crossing.
Keep eyes peeled for Joe Blakes.
Sheds, woodstacks, porch entrances,
the backs of properties only ever seen from the front.
Sniff out Main Road.
The crunch of slipping stones as you climb
in full sun, past netted fruit trees until
bitumen.

Poppies

meet sunshine
on their own terms
brush against
each other
blamelessly
glad handle air

green

I need green
all shades of it

still green
shifting green

see-through green
solid green

sun-speckled green
shaded green

green tending to yellow
green hinting at blue

sleek green
variegated green

glossy green
fat flat green

climbing green
horizontal green

sprouting green
established green

garden green
even weed green

green permitting other colours
greedy green

a kiss

shut up
lean in
full tilt
mouth probe
face to
face two
speak not
talk tongue
lip cling
let mind
unplug
how long
not yet

double take

passing a parked car
I see the grimacing face
and tensed upper arms
of a man mowing
his nature strip

drawing away
the rear-view mirror reveals
my mistake
the man is pushing twins
in a double pusher

haiku

at dusk
a windflower closes
your visit

ground control
sends up signal wafts
hyacinths

caught snow
on bare black branches
– blossom

in the garden
shadow boxing the breeze
daffodils

the chough's head
darting around like
a sprinkler nozzle

the live sherrin

leaps with latent energy
pops and darts
fizzes from fingers
until

the line is crossed

at which time it becomes
a dead thing
lolls
on its stitching

but hurled back
onto the live surface
it charges and spits
defies evenness
of bounce

attracts addicts
lures live flesh
calls

more of me more more
flick me kick me
punch me
celebrate my arc

land me
lace out
in soft hands
send me straight
between the big ones

Long on

Dud fieldsmen get captain-directed right
down on the fence, miles from close-in slips
action, where the favoured lap up the sass
and chat between balls.

At change of overs, you either bolt
down the other end or get slight relief
by holding down mid-off for an over
where at least voices are audible.

Once in a blue googly, someone swats
a sitter to you in close and if you manage
to dispel your panic and actually swallow
the catch, you will know true gratitude.

Normally restrained leggies and offies,
unlike their wild-haired, truculent
cousin quicks, will gather you up,
tousle your hair and grin goofily,

pretending they planned the trap.
But mostly, fielding is a lonely business,
hearing distant thunks as the cherry
arcs off where others congregate.

Late in the innings, you may be offered
another reprieve, closer to the popping
crease but equally isolated – deep fine
leg – on the off chance of picking up

a skewed hook or a keeper's miss.
On TV, balls glide across bowling green-
like surfaces but in the suburbs, any-
thing can happen as balls fizz and jump

over mis-mown, crevice-cracked buffalo
grass. A sweep along the ground can
leap up and collect you in the teeth.
But must not fray your focus. Just don't

let that ball get to the boundary.
You're there for the duration
of the afternoon, holding down
a position. Sorts you, fielding.

tangling

anybody
can untangle
find the narrow end
chase it back

what takes pluck
is tangling
seek a host
commence to bind

shoot for the sky
embrace thick and thin
enmesh the unaware
capture

be bold but subtle
don't announce
your takeover bid
colonise some trunk

but send outliers on
delicate wrapping missions
and when you win
don't stop

enswathe yourself
keep going
tangling the very air
then flower

untrue grit

when you're outside
and feel a bit of grit
between your toes
you sit

untie your bootlace
peel off your sock
turn it inside out
take stock

find nothing much
it doesn't seem fair
it felt like
something was there

in lockdown
for something else to do
try inserting
some grit in your shoe

Found

Came upon a search party
heading up Mt Discovery at dusk.
Looked like a task for Vaclav
to lend a hand.

As darkness claimed trees
the swish of footsteps slowed
until torches cut into the dark
and the first voices rang out.

Vaclav! Vaclav!
Where are you?
I stopped mid-stride,
turned and flung back my hood,

switched the torchbeam full
on my face.
It's me. I'm here.
I've found me.

sadness

i

sadness lies still
even when stirred

settling silently
unshareably

its source
and purpose

elusive as the dreams
of a sleeping lizard

sadness opens up
into a wall-less cavern

its low hum
all-penetrating

ii

sadness is solitary
a personalised
looming

sadness can be thin
and distant
a retreating carriage

or sumptuous
the full
spread

a deep
enveloping
reservoir

iii

from somewhere
sadness adds a dimension
even if we struggle
to recognise it

a state
of neutrality
a climate
for consideration

worlds from the chimera
of engagement
sadness perforates
what passes for contentment

Plane speaking

As I watch my father dressing
a piece of wood clamped tight
in his bench vice,
eyes trained on the blade path,
he allows me a slice of thought.

You know, he begins,
voice finding its groove,
as wood shavings continue
to pool at his feet,
and before long, I do.

Ray's

Just got to pop round to Ray's
for a minute to see if he might
have a tail light for the trailer.

Ray's: quaint that Dad would still
so refer to his local service station.
Ray Molloy used to race Minis,

a cheeky, grease-faced loon.
Sold me my first car: a crimson
Morry 1100. Lasted six months.

Ray'd shaken his head. Con-rod's
shot right through the back
of the manifold. It's buggered,

he said. You're lucky: I've got
another one in the yard. He did too.
White, rusty, peeling duco

but the engine was toey-er
than my red one. Might be worth
transferring it to the better body.

Or I could just have it as is,
for $100. Red one never got
a look-in. I slapped on the P's.

Now, some old guy limps
out to Dad, shakes his head.
Jim, they don't make bulbs

like this any more. Could try
Bunnings I suppose. Feel free
to put some air in those tyres.

Dad's put 30 in one and started
phffting about on the other
when the old guy shambles over

with a dusty packet and a screwdriver.
Might just give this one a go for you.
Sure enough, the long globe

does the trick. How much?
Oh, five bucks. Dad looks
at me. I take out a fiver

from my wallet. You remember
my boy Bill, Ray? Hell,
it IS Ray, just fleshier, slower.

He doesn't even look up,
just finishes screwing. You
sold me my first car, I say.

Know what he did for his 75th
birthday last year, Dad asks,
eyes on the road.

Took a cruise. Down the Rhine.
Ray's petrol always was dearer.
I used to go to the Caltex

over the road. Now Ray's stands alone. And over the road looms a six-storey apartment block.

Nailman

Tuh-tap-tap. Waap. Four blows
and the three-inch nail was flush.
That's counting the set-up tap.

When the power goes off now
on a building site, carpenters
knock off for the day.

In Jim's time, you just
got on with it. Power
was for the sparkies.

Stripped to the waist,
cracked leather tool bag
aproning his faded shorts,

Jim put in steady days
on Bendigo housing blocks,
armed with his smooth,

wooden-handled hammer
and nail punch, black-handled
builder's square rammed

in his belt, flick-hinged
carpenter's rule at the ready
and stubby, flat, red pencil.

A portable one-man constructor.
Even as I homeworked
over a desk as a teenager,

on weekends, I knew
his presence, nails jangling
in that tool bag, interspersed

with regular hammer blows,
some backyard project
always on the go.

The fete on a Saturday
at the local grammar school,
saw well-heeled mothers,

cardiganed fathers and kids
haggling for bargains. Away
from trimmed doilies and napkins,

a makeshift sideshow
offered a pound note
to anyone who could drive

a nail into thick board
in five or fewer blows.
I had to insist.

Jim bought Choc Wedges
for the family, all five of us.
Proud, was I, as punch.

The Quiet Shop

Slices of silence for sale.
All winter stock must go.

Peaceful pieces, snow-hushed
layers of deepest absorption.

Complete clearance. Snap
up soundless bargains.

Make us a mute offer.
We'll be all eyes.

New spring stock
arriving next week:

low utterances
and whispers are back

The task

As dusk threatened to steal what light remained
she hacked at grass on the drive with the old straw broom

Her father had insisted she finish before dinner
but each stroke seemed to sweep the deadline off

Clippings careered from concrete but only as far
as the upright blades forming the lawn border

more often bouncing back onto the drive
She turned and whisked again the wayward grass

But try as she might some dogged specks resisted
Dad will never come at this she knew

So while the light survived a little longer
she tossed the broom and got down on her knees

and on the final darkening square – she blew
until the grassy shreds rejoined live lawn

But how could she be sure she wondered now
as path and lawn assumed a matching shade

What's this I feel crawling across my face
her fleeing thought as the outside light snapped on

Lady Time

For all the glory of her parade
Lady Time goes about her business
soundlessly, colourlessly

Winged thief she may be
but she cares not a tock
for moments stolen

Such lucre
simply pocketed
as her procession moves on

Incapable of stillness
she is perpeptual
untouchable

issuing webs of attachment
and withdrawing such links
so gradually that

flashes of the past
even embalmed memories
suddenly find themselves

untethered to tempo
scrambling for sequence
and mindholds

When David Bowie Died

Cockatoos screeched high in the air,
a white manna gum bough cracked like a shot,
the report echoing down Doctor's Gully before it crunched
to earth. Surviving branches sprang back, shaking.

The Essendon Football Club
was wiped out by decree,
Jerry Hall accepted living
hell with Rupert Murdoch.

And near dusk, a small
perfectly formed rainbow
stood to attention
behind the Savoia Hotel.

The long goodbye

Volume only goes so far –
there comes a morning
when the shampoo bottle
propped upside down
in the shower cubicle
so the last of its substance
can be squeezed out
blows
from its nozzle
nothing
but whistling air

the door handle

preliminary
to push
or pull

quiet cousin
of tongue
and lock

turning
barrier
into passage

Roger stoops

A feather
floats
in his gaze
almost as if he has willed it into being.
First the hollow shaft, the calamus,
dips,
then pops up,
allowing the top end of the rachis
to take its playful downward turn
and on
and down
like a tiny skiff in a dancing sea
until it settles on the blue court.

Roger's eyes have followed it all the way
to its soft, silent landing.
Now he steps over the baseline,
drops to one knee,
picks up the feather between thumb and forefinger,
and deposits it behind the playing area.
The ref allows the delay.
His opponent fumes.

That's all it takes.
He wins his service game,
calmly returns anything sent his way
and accepts the match,
does Roger Featherer.

Prophylactic days

People are still there
mostly
but the enforced distance is, well,
distancing

In some ways
it might be easier if they weren't,
there, I mean
There'd still be contact memory

Feels like you are talking
to your past
to a veneer of person
you once engaged with

A dimension is missing
Where once you 3D-ed
now your life is screened,
offering more like two

When you see a friend
on the street, you adopt
a position of regard,
feet foxing on the footpath

Conscious of personal
space intrusions
you may find yourself
speaking a little louder

senryu 2

coronavirus –
a pink dogwood leaf
catches the breeze

closer
to his neighbour
the new fence

opinions
form and gush
the Hepburn blowhole

a flash of yellow
between the damp trees
the postie's raincoat

insomnia…
lying here
knots leaping

European wasps

seem to form into being
out of the very air

following invisible trajectories
to the front of their nest

where they pull up
as if the power has just been turned off

Bark

Sound of a thick dry ribbon of pink bark scraping
high up in the candlebark. Uneven gusts of wind.
One swirl soon, the tatter will snap.

Parting from attachments can be a wrench.
And after breakaway, that feeling,
silently floating

Word purchasing

What if Spotify got its mitts on books?
Not online book orders or Kindling
What if you could buy books
the way you do music now?
Eschewing whole titles
set in the the creator's order
what if you only selected
choice cuts?

Cut to the chase
Do not go gentle
No need to enter the fullness
of that good night

Pluck a paragraph
from *Les Mis* –
a Cosette riverside ramble
or a juicy chapter –
say Jean Valjean's interrogation
by that faux Waterloo soldier

Take more War or more Peace
Your choice
Less rhetoric
and once you're done
tampering with Tolstoy
why not shrivel Shakespeare
cherry pick Chekhov
fillet Flaubert

Play them back to yourself
these selections
the part indicative of the whole
Who has time?
Just milk the word cream
and on your bookshelves
hard drives
think
of the space you'll save

But don't stop there
Lovingly curate
Pay not by the word
but by the letter
The Color Purple
US edition will save you
the cost of a vowel

Explosion

So spontaneously does her laugh sputter up that an unlit cigarette springs from her lips and lands longitudinally on her pulsing lap. On the bounce, she captures the cigarette in a light fist and waits for her body to catch up.

Why are ducks funny?

Speak of sparrows, storks, wrens,
cockies, prowling great eagles
and you won't get a grin.
But ducks, especially on land,
are just funny.

They move awkwardly,
that swaying, skew-whiff motion as if
they just invented it –
even the word waddle
is chucklesome.

Granted they appear
to move with grace in water,
gliding along the surface
splashlessly
but get a gander
at what's going on beneath –
that egg-beater action,
with those short legs
and comical webbed feet
which are orange!

And what about that arced bill,
spatulate and flat
and sort of smug-looking?
OK it helps with filtering
and foraging for food
but it just looks
gooby.

Now what if you felt like
shooting the breeze
with a duck?
Well, if you cop a drake,
you'll find him silent
as the tomb
but Mrs Duck may well
grant you a grunt,
a groan, a chirp
or even a squeak
but very few actually quack.
Doesn't matter.
Some do
so the lot are tarbrushed.

Disney's Donald may have tried
to dignify ducks,
Scrooge dipped his lid to Dickens
but the eternal duck
will always be
Daffy.

yellow leaves

two sweaty men in yellow vests
here for the piano, meant to be on the veranda
the cherry tree branch leaned over the drive
japanese guests had admired the pink blossom

here for the piano, meant to be on the veranda
better than japan, too much pollution now
japanese guests had admired the pink blossom
three months of no rain to speak of

better than japan, too much pollution now
not sure if the leaves are changing or dying
three months of no rain to speak of
and then the leaves were yellow

not sure if the leaves are changing or dying
removals truck backs down the drive
and the leaves were yellow
and the broken branch hung limp

no piano here, mate, be careful reversing
the cherry tree branch leaned over the drive
kookaburra laughs in the old gum tree
two sweaty men in yellow vests

Daylesford

A bristling block of almost city
jammed with hipster cafés, hair salons,
bookshops, galleries, retro furniturers,
fine wool and wine shops, smart cars
and forever-tarting-up, the rump Rex theatre
Daylesford eases off to country at either end.

Two glistening fountains bracket the strip,
one gothic-lit down the post office end,
one at full splash near the mower shop,
viewable from a corner table at the Taj.
And always, volcanic-soiled Wombat Hill
looms over the convent's grand balconies.

Follow brick-red kiss-me-quicks, pale jonquils
bluebells, Swiss-Italian planted pines,
elms, red oaks, birches, copper beeches,
flaky-ribboned manna gums and candle barks
along grassed gullies and steep ridges
and soon you land in gentle Hepburn Springs.

Chimneys ease woodsmoke at dusk,
bagged horse poo sells at the side of the road.
Ivy advances on fading guest houses
but new street trees are coming soon.
Merv still serves rissoles at the Savoia,
where the bottleshop bell rings in the bar.

Trains trickle to Bullarto once a week.
Sunday markets surge and annual parades
release floats and tractors and firetrucks.
Black ice slicks up the road in winter,
the cold seems to go on forever but all
are welcome under the regional Rainbow.

Remembrance Day

Detour in Daylesford.
Flagman on the job.

Marchers heading over
from the RSL

to the memorial mini park
– traffic island really.

So slowly they move
these old warriors

with their red poppies.
Choosing not to march at all,

one watches from his standing point
in the front beer garden,

crunching loudly
on chips

as he removes them in loose
formation from foil.

On the blink

I'll just, I think,
pull in here
and get some petrol,
must have a Coles docket somewhere.

I'm soo ooo ooh
tired,
sings John Lennon,
my mind is on the blink.

Switch off the car,
the Beatles.

Go to click
the petrol cap,
not the cap,
the bit of car body
covering the petrol cap.
Hesitate.

Pop.

The bonnet jumps.
Get out. Clunk it back down.
Reach around under
the steering wheel.
Pop.
Bonnet again.

Bright sunshine all round.
I've had the Sooby eight years.
Bought it new.

I wonder should I call you
But I know what you would do
You'd say I'm putting you on
But it's no joke,
is it John.

Bloke ahead has pulled out now.
I start the car,
follow him out.

Back home in the carport,
I push the door to get out,
drop the keys.
Look down between the seat and the door.
Keys on the petrol catch release jigger.

Breakdown

How do they know, things,
to read momentum
and start breaking down?

The front bushes on the Impreza
are worn, I'm told, and not
like a shirt,

uneven tyre wear the giveaway.
But what's that got to do
with air conditioning on the blink

or a rusted-out whatsit
in the hydronic heating boiler,
an iPod that no longer syncs,

an aromatic daphne
shedding its bark,
a pair of old jeans just deciding

to go at the knee,
the knees themselves
calling time on garden squatting?

Some inaudible hoy
must have been given
and the unravelling begins.

Soap

A year of used soaps
an art installation featuring
slightly differently shaped soaplets
each allotted a tiny shelf
in the soaparama

An environmental hello perhaps
but surely most of us
are not so profligate
Seeing a soap so whittled
as to offer inadequate lather
don't we simply attach it
to a ripe new soap
and allow the soap juices
to do their cling thing

the grip tentative at first
even by shower's end
but by next morning
we behold
a conglomerate soap

and what is interesting
is that the original worn-down item
will still carry on getting smaller
each day
until you realise
it has disappeared entirely

Did the nub wear out faster
or has it been absorbed
into the new soap?

Each day as we add
experiences to our lives
how many smooth into our being
how many slip away
never gaining purchase
how many
remain uncertainly
lumped to us?

Time out

Time to sort out this watch
It's been losing time now
for months
or just plain stopping
I presume it's the battery

No one in Daylesford will do it
Castlemaine jewellers require
a morning drop-off
and late afternoon collection
I don't have that much time

I ring Mr Minit in Ballarat
How long I ask
to change a watch battery
Seconds he says
I'll be there

In the promised seconds
he's done it
but he's frowning
Problem with the second hand
It's not going now

You can take it to my boss
if you like in Wendouree
Google maps' vocalist
rhymes the lake suburb
with dowry rather than debris

No seconds man the boss
Give me twenty minutes says he
I'm back short of that probably
because how can I tell
My wrist is blank

The mechanism is fine
It's Seiko but –
and here he taps a tiny copper rod
and says something or other
and then something else

I know the drill
Replace expensive innards
or buy a new item
He points down the arcade
Prouds is just over there

How much time have I got
We don't says Cormac McCarthy
move through days / they move
through us / the passing of time
is irrevocably the passing of you

I can of course scrabble around
in my pocket for the phone
but I miss my skin companion
Uncalibrated time moving through me
feels like strange limbo

Acknowledgements

The A.R. Ammons poem 'When I was young the silk' was partly a springboard for 'The driveway'.

'The footy' and 'the live sherrin' have appeared online in *The Footy Almanac, 2022.*

'Prophylactic days' was a prize-winning poem in the *Trentham Words in Winter* Poetry Competition, 2020.

'tangling', 'Green', 'untrue grit', 'Breakdown', 'On the blink' and the haiku beginning 'in the garden' have appeared in 'Local Lines' in *The Local* (editor and director, Donna Kelly).

The senryu which begins, 'coronavirus – ' appeared in *failed haiku: A Journal of English Haiku*, 2021.

The senyru which begins 'closer' was accepted for publication in *Frog Pond, Journal of the Haiku Society of America,* spring/summer issue 45:2, 2022.

www.ingramcontent.com/pod-product-compliance
Lightning Source LLC
Chambersburg PA
CBHW070336120526
44590CB00017B/2905
* 9 7 8 1 7 6 1 0 9 5 2 1 4 *